PRAYING IN THE
FRANCISCAN SPIRIT

SISTER FRANCES TERESA, OSC

First published in 1999 by
KEVIN MAYHEW LTD
Buxhall
Stowmarket
Suffolk IP30 3BW

ISBN 1 84003 438 6
Catalogue No 1500313

Front cover: *Hands of an Apostle*, 1508
(brush drawing) by Albrecht Durer (1471-1528).
Graphische Sammlung Albertina, Vienna/Bridgeman
Art Library, London/New York.

Background: *Poppies* by Alan Bedding

Cover design: Angela Palfrey
Editor: Helen Elliot
Typesetting: Richard Weaver

Printed and bound in Great Britain

CONTENTS

*To Francis and Clare
and all the great Franciscans
who have taught me so much –
thank you.*

Introduction

Francis (Francesco Bernadone) was born in 1181 or 1182, the son of a wealthy cloth merchant who had many connections with France, which is why he wanted his son called Francesco. Francis was the natural leader of the Assisi youth, but gradually became overwhelmed by a divine restlessness. After long and painful uncertainty, he went into the ruined chapel of San Damiano to pray before the crucifix, and there Christ spoke to him: 'Francis, repair my house which, as you can see, is falling into ruins.'

Misunderstanding this, Francis started to rebuild the walls of the chapel, using money raised by selling cloth from his father's warehouse. While rebuilding, he was overtaken by the prophetic knowledge that one day holy women would live there. 'He spoke of us' said Clare, years later. Clare was a young, beautiful aristocrat from Assisi who was moved by the same divine inspiration as Francis.

Soon after this, Francis was taken to court by his father for misappropriation of goods. He responded by stripping off his clothes and handing them back, claiming utter dependence on his Father in heaven. He and Clare began to meet secretly, and on Palm Sunday 1212, she left her home at night to join Francis and the brothers who had gathered round him. Francis cut off her long, fair hair and she promised him obedience, a promise which she kept faithfully.

Because they were both fired by a vision of Gospel life, and fiercely drawn to the human person of Jesus, large numbers of men and women came to join them. Francis' brotherhood rapidly expanded to hundreds, not all of whom genuinely shared his ideals, a fact which led to much pain and conflict. Clare's sisters grew in number, too, and at her death over 250 communities of women looked to her as their leader.

Both Francis and Clare sought to put God, as revealed in the poverty of Christ, at the heart of their lives, living simply and as brother and sister to all that exists. They recognised that when God is central, all creation will find its proper place. Their spirituality is marked by simplicity and intensity, deep insights into the cross and an understanding of the glory that is ours in Christ. They loved poverty as the road to Christ and as the answer to greed and materialism. They had no wish to compound the problems they saw in their society. They owned no property and refused positions of honour in the Church.

The Rule of St Francis is based on two Scriptural texts:

These twelve Jesus sent out, instructing them as follows: . . . Provide yourselves with no gold or silver, not even with coppers for your purses (Matthew 10:5, 9).

If anyone wants to be a follower of mine, let him renounce himself and take up his cross every day, and follow me (Luke 9:23).

Towards the end of his life, Francis' years of prayer and devotion to the suffering Christ brought him to the strange mystery of the stigmata, when the wounds of Christ appeared on his own body. Two years later, in 1226, he died, and was canonised in1228 by Pope Gregory IX. Clare lived on for nearly thirty years, a visible example of their Gospel ideal, a faithful lover of the Lord, living to the end the Gospel she had embraced so young. She was the first woman in history to write a rule for other women, one of such balance and simplicity that it is still observed today by her daughters, the Poor Clares.

FRANCIS AND CLARE

In 1209 or 1210, the young Francis of Assisi was in great psychological and spiritual turmoil and anguish. His former values no longer satisfied him but his new value system had not yet been revealed. He wandered around the hills of Assisi, following the paths beneath his feet, longing for guidance and, unknown to himself, undergoing profound inner changes. He says of this time:

> No one showed me what I should do, but the Most High Himself revealed to me that I should live according to the form of the Holy Gospel. *Testament of Francis*

One day, Francis heard this passage from the Gospel read:

> As you go, proclaim that the kingdom of heaven is close at hand. Cure the sick, raise the dead, cleanse lepers, cast out devils. You received without charge, give without charge. Provide yourselves with no gold or silver, not even a few coppers for your purses, with no haversack for the journey, no spare tunic or footwear or staff, for the workman deserves his keep.
> *Matthew 10:6-10*

He recognised his own call within this, and cried out:

This is what I wish, this is what I seek, this is what I long to do with all my heart.

1 Celano 22
(the official biographer of Francis)

Francis grew rapidly in love for Jesus. One day, walking near Assisi, he went, on an impulse of the Spirit, into the little ruined ninth-century chapel of San Damiano.

An inner voice invited him to pray and a tender compassionate voice then spoke to him: 'Francis, do you not see that my house is falling into ruin? Go and repair it for me.' Trembling and amazed, Francis replied: 'Gladly I will do so, O Lord.' He had understood that the Lord was speaking of that very church which, on account of its age, was indeed falling into ruin.

These words filled him with the greatest joy and inner light, because in spirit he knew it was indeed Jesus Christ who had spoken to him . . . From that hour his heart was stricken and wounded with melting love and compassion for the passion of

Christ; and for the rest of his life he carried in it the wounds of the Lord Jesus. This was clearly proved later when the stigmata of those same wounds were miraculously impressed upon his holy body for all to see.

The Legend of the Three Companions

Clare was later to tell us:

Almost immediately after his conversion, while he had neither brothers nor companions, when he was building the Church of San Damiano in which he was totally filled with divine consolation, he was led to abandon the world completely. This holy man, in the great joy and enlightenment of the Holy Spirit, made a prophecy about us which the Lord fulfilled later. Climbing the wall of that church he shouted in French to some poor people who were standing nearby: 'Come and help me build the monastery of San Damiano, because ladies will. dwell here who will glorify our heavenly Father throughout his whole Church by their celebrated and holy manner of life.'

Testament of Clare

An anonymous thirteenth-century Franciscan said this of Clare:

It is a mystery that God on the same day created for the first man 'a helper as his partner', because God also made for Blessed Francis 'a helper as his partner' from his side, that is from his own people, from his own town. This is the most blessed virgin Clare, who can truly be called woman, that is acting strongly, because her virtuous deeds, shining with the clear light of the virtues, light up this world with a wondrous light.

A meditation in solitude of one who is poor

Francis and Clare often used to say this prayer:

O God, sublime and glorious,
    come and enlighten
    the darkness of my heart;
    give me an honest faith,
    a firm hope
    and a perfect love;
    by your gift
    may I feel and know

your holy will,
that I may obey it
and not go astray.

Another ancient prayer which they both loved is still said by Franciscans when they begin and end their time of prayer. Francis used to say it wherever he was, on the roads, sitting by the hedgerows, in a chapel, anywhere:

We adore you, most holy Lord Jesus
    Christ,
  here and in all your churches in the
    whole world,
  and we bless you
  because by your holy cross,
  you have redeemed the world.

OUR LONGINGS
AND OUR STRUGGLES

Francis believed that poverty, humility and simplicity would teach him and his brothers how to imitate the Son of God, Jesus, in his human life.

He used to say:

> I recommend to you these three things:
> first simplicity, to counteract the excessive thirst for knowledge;
> secondly prayer, which the devil is always trying to hinder by various means;
> thirdly, love of poverty and holy Poverty herself.   *Fioretti*

While Clare would say:

> Desire to have above all else the Spirit of the Lord and his holy manner of working.
> *Clare: Rule*

Francis wrote an Office of the Passion which he and Clare used frequently. In it, he put together texts and his own thoughts to create his own psalms.

I will praise you, Lord,
  most holy Father, king of heaven and
    earth,
  for you have consoled me.
You are God my Saviour,
  I will act confidently and not be afraid.

The Lord is my strength and my glory,
  he has become my salvation.
Your right hand, O Lord, is magnificent in
    strength,
  your right hand, O Lord, has shattered
    the enemy,
  and in the vastness of your glory
  you have overthrown my enemies.
Let the poor see this and be glad;
  seek God and your soul shall live.
Let heaven and earth praise him,
  the sea and every living thing in them.

A psalm for times of distress
How long, O Lord, will you eternally
  forget me?
How long will you turn your face from me?
How long must I place doubts in my soul,
  sorrow in my heart each day?

How long will my enemy rejoice over me?
Look and hear me, O Lord my God.
Give light to my eyes
  that I may never sleep in death,
  that my enemy may never say:
  I have overcome him.
Those who trouble me would rejoice if I
  stumbled,
    but I have trusted in your kindness.

My heart shall rejoice in your saving help,
  I will sing to the Lord who has given
    good things to me,
  and I will praise the name of the Lord
    most high.

We are told that Francis struggled for many years with a temptation and seemed to be making no progress. One day, almost in despair, he was praying about this temptation, and heard a voice saying:

'Francis, if you have faith like a mustard seed, you will say to this mountain: "Remove from here, and it will remove".' Francis said: 'What mountain, Lord?' and again he heard: 'The mountain is your temptation.' Weeping, Francis said: 'Let it be as you have said', and immediately the temptation was driven out and he was made free and put completely at peace with himself.

2 Celano 115
(called The Remembrance of
the Desires of a Soul)

THE LORD'S PRAYER

*Francis wrote a paraphrase on the Our Father,
which can still warm us with his fervour:*

OUR FATHER MOST HOLY,
   our Creator and Redeemer,
   our Saviour and Consoler.

WHO ART IN HEAVEN,
   in the angels and saints,
   enlightening them that they may know
      you,
   for you, Lord, are the light;
   enkindling them that they may love you,
   for you, Lord, are love;
   dwelling in them
   and filling them with your divinity,
   that bliss may be theirs,
   for you, Lord, are the highest Good,
   the eternal Good, from whom all goodness
      flows,
   without whom nothing is good.

YOUR NAME BE HELD HOLY:
   may our knowledge of you
   shine ever more clearly within us

that we may perceive
the breadth of your blessings,
the extent of your promises,
the height of your majesty,
the depth of your judgements.

YOUR KINGDOM COME:
rule us now, through grace,
and bring us at last to your Kingdom of
light
where we shall see you as you are,
and our love for you will be made perfect,
our union blissful,
our joy unending in you.

YOUR WILL BE DONE ON EARTH AS IN HEAVEN:
may we love you:
with all our heart,
ever thinking of you;
with all our soul,
ever longing for you;
with all our mind,
directing all our aims to you
and seeking nothing but your glory;
with all our strength,
spending all our energies
and all our senses of soul and body
to serve only your love and nothing else.

May we love our neighbours as ourselves:
  drawing them all to your love
  in so far as we can,
  sharing their good fortune
  as if it were our own,
  helping them to bear their trials
  and doing them no wrong.

GIVE US THIS DAY OUR DAILY BREAD,
  your beloved Son
  our Lord Jesus Christ,
  that we may remember,
  understand and revere
  the love he showed for us
  and all he said and did and suffered
  for our sake.

FORGIVE US OUR SINS
  through your mercy beyond words,
  through the power of the passion
  of your beloved Son,
  through the merits and intercession
  of the Virgin Mary
  and of all your chosen ones.

AS WE FORGIVE THOSE WHO SIN AGAINST US
  and that we ourselves cannot fully forgive,
  make us fully forgive;

make us love our enemies
truly, for your sake;
teach us how to pray sincerely
to you on their behalf;
and not to render harm for harm
to anyone, but rather try
to do good to all, in you!

AND LEAD US NOT INTO TEMPTATION
whether veiled or visible,
sudden or searing or prolonged.

BUT DELIVER US FROM EVIL
past, present and to come. Amen.

*Francis**

*Francis also wrote this prayer for his and
Clare's companions to say before each part of
the Divine Office, the Church's liturgical prayer:*

God, all-powerful, most holy,
sublime ruler of all,
you alone are good –
supremely good, fully, completely good;
may we render to you all praise,
all glory, all thanksgiving,
all honour and all blessing;
may we always ascribe to you alone
everything that is good. Amen.

*Francis**

FOLLOWERS OF
FRANCIS AND CLARE

Anthony of Padua, a Portuguese, joined Francis in 1219, after meeting the first friars going to Morocco. Later their bodies were brought back to his monastery. Both these encounters made a deep impression on Anthony. He was much loved by Francis, who called him 'Anthony, my bishop'. Anthony was a gifted and deeply pastoral preacher who also wrote a number of prayers for people to use. His ministry was full of wonders and cures, and he is still much loved, far beyond the boundaries of the Church, not least for his skill in finding things that are lost.

Holy Spirit
> you who are the love of the Father and
> the Son,
> let your love cover the multitude of our
> sins.
To you be honour and glory
> through all ages. Amen.
> > *St Anthony Sermons I/364*

You ought to have external peace with your neighbour; internal peace with yourself; eternal peace with God.

We beg you, Holy Spirit,
  pour out the salve of your mercy
  like the good Samaritan
  on the wounds of our soul.
Bind them with the bandages of your
  grace,
    mount our souls on the pack animal of
      obedience,
    lead us to the shelter of conversion:
    entrust us to the care of contrition
    so that we may rest a long time under
      your protection
    until we recover our lost salvation
    with the money of true sorrow.
After having found it
  grant that we may have the strength
  to return along the road that leads to
    you
  from which we strayed.
With your help, Amen.

St Anthony Sermons II/191

*Another great follower of Francis was
Bonaventure, later Cardinal and, later still,
Minister General of the Friars Minor. Legend
has it that, as a child, Bonaventure had been
cured by Francis. He did much to resolve the
conflicting currents among the brothers. He
was a close friend of Thomas Aquinas when*

they were both teaching at the university in Paris. Despite his elevation to Cardinal, Bonaventure remained a man of deep, even mystical, prayer. This is reflected in his writings, particularly the Journey of the Soul into God, *a wonderful map of our spiritual wanderings.*

> Feed us with your fruits;
>   shed light upon our thoughts.
> Lead us along straight paths.
> Crush the attacks of the enemy.
> Fill us with your sacred light;
>   breathe holy inspiration;
>   be a peaceful way of life
>   for those who fear Christ. Amen.
>
> *Bonaventure: Tree of Life*

Francis gave Brother Leo a lesson once which teaches all Franciscans how lightly we should sit to the good and pleasant things of this world. In fact he goes further and suggests that the Gospel offers us a complete reversal of values, one which we find today no easier than Brother Leo found then. Francis said to him:

> When we come to St Mary of the Angels, soaked by rain and frozen by the cold, all soiled with mud and suffering from hunger, and we ring at the gate and the brother

porter comes and says angrily: 'Who are you?' and we say: 'We are two of your brothers,' and he contradicts us, saying: 'You are not telling the truth. Rather you are two rascals who go around deceiving people and stealing what they give to the poor. Go away!' and he does not open for us, but makes us stand outside in the snow and rain, cold and hungry, until night falls – then if we endure all those insults and cruel rebuffs patiently without being troubled and without complaining, and if we reflect humbly and charitably that that porter really knows us and that God makes him speak against us, oh Brother Leo, write that perfect joy is there!

Fioretti 8

Angela of Foligno was a second-generation follower of Francis and Clare. A lay woman, she lived an intense spiritual life, having some extraordinary experiences, and wrote a fascinating study of prayer and account of her own journey which has much to teach us today.

On Maundy Thursday I was meditating on the death of the incarnate Son of God and striving to empty my mind of everything else. Suddenly while I was in this effort and desire, a divine word sounded in my soul: 'I have not loved you in jest.' And this word struck me a mortal blow. I understood the perfect truth of what he said, namely that it was not in jest but by a most perfect and tender love that he had loved me.

Angela of Foligno: Writings nos. 238, 374
(A fourteenth-century Franciscan Tertiary)

Present-day Franciscans continue to reflect on this difficult reversal of values and to write prayers and meditations which struggle with the way we live the Gospel today.

If I were to speak in the tongue of curias and diplomats,
  and were rich in knowledge but poor in wisdom;
  if I were to prefer the logic of power to the logic of a vulnerable blossom,
  I would become but withered wood and a shrivelled flower.
But the fruits of the Spirit are sensitivity, self-criticism,
  humour, recognition of one's own limitations,
  unconditional solidarity with the powerless,
  but also the ability to distinguish

when a person's survival depends on a
   piece of bread,
and when for the poor it is rather
a rose or a gentle melody that is important.

Br Gilles, OFM
(A twentieth-century Friar)

*A twentieth-century Poor Clare makes the
same prayer in simple terms. The sister was
over 90 when she wrote this, the distillation
of many years' thought and prayer.*

Dear Lord
   Hear me.
   Heed me.
   Help me.
   Hold me.
   Hide me.
   Hearten me.
   Hush me.
   And be heaven to me.

M. Austin, OSC
(A twentieth-century Poor Clare)

*What is the attraction which Francis and Clare
have for people today? In May 1999, over
70,000 young people walked to Assisi on a
pilgrimage for peace. For them, Francis is a
leader, an inspiration, a living person who sill
teaches and guides. He speaks directly to us*

on so many of today's burning issues: peace; brotherhood and sisterhood; living in harmony with our planet, with nature, with our neighbour; he speaks about a simple lifestyle in which we are content to have what we need and to share with those around us.

He and Clare also speak to us about a way of living in which men and women share something much richer than sexual experience and in which they are no longer at war. In spite of the very real sufferings of both their lives, they speak to us about joy, happiness, delight in God and creation, about living together in peace and concord. They were both peacemakers, they were both challenging, they were both intense lovers of God and of those around them. Even today, they continue to do what they did in their lifetime – to draw us onward to fulfil the true greatness that is in us by helping us to discover the joy of being little, of being lesser, of being powerless.

Because they still speak to us so powerfully, many people still want to be, in some way, under their protection. Recently, Clare has come much more to the foreground. It seems as if she has a gift for today, perhaps especially for the women of today, but she also bears gifts of prayer and a reminder of our need for a contemplative dimension in our lives. She seems to be doing for men and women of today what she did for Francis and the early friars – she reminds us about the values of prayer and contemplation and the inner, intangible things of the heart. As a result, Franciscan groups are still being formed, some along old models, some taking completely new forms. Ever since Francis' own time, there have been groups of lay people who followed his values, living in poverty and peace. Today the Secular Franciscan Order still flourishes around the world. They say that only God really knows how many Franciscans there are.

JESUS' HUMANITY
AND OUR HUMANITY

Down the ages, Franciscans have learnt from Francis and Clare how to find their desires and struggles, their weakness and their greatness mirrored in the humanity of Jesus. Like Francis, Clare pondered daily on the crucifix. With their followers, she and Francis teach us to enter into Jesus' redemptive suffering and death:

If so great and good a Lord, then, on coming into the virgin's womb, chose to appear despised, needy and poor in this world so that people who were in utter poverty and want and in absolute need of heavenly nourishment, might become rich in him by possessing the kingdom of heaven, then rejoice and be glad! Be filled with a remarkable happiness and spiritual joy!

Clare, first letter to Agnes of Prague

Gaze on him,
consider him
contemplate him
as you desire to imitate him.

Clare, second letter to Agnes of Prague

31

Look upon that mirror every day and continually study your face in it, so that you may adorn yourself, within and without, with beautiful robes, and cover yourself with the flowers and garments of all the virtues. Indeed, blessed poverty, holy humility and ineffable charity are reflected in that mirror.

Clare, fourth letter to Agnes of Prague

A prayer of total self-giving

I beg you, Lord,
let the fiery, gentle power
of your love
take possession of my soul,
and snatch it away
from everything under heaven,
that I may die
for love of your love,
as you saw fit to die
for love of mine. Amen.

*Francis**

Lord Jesus, make of us
good and fertile soil
to receive the seeds of your grace,
and make it yield worthy fruits of penance
so that with your help

we may live eternally in your glory,
you who are blessed throughout all ages.
Amen.   *St Anthony, Sermons I/37*

Out of love for us, Jesus bound himself so
tightly to us that his love took on our agony as
his own, as if he could not wish to remain in
heaven without us.

Christ our Lord
we ask you humbly
to gather us under the wings of your love.
Keep us alive
with the water of remorse,
the air of contemplation,
the fire of love
and the earth of humility,
so that we may join you, who are life itself
and blessed through all ages. Amen.
                    St Anthony, Sermons II/394

A fish is not hurt by the constant pounding of the
sea, nor is faith destroyed by life's adversities.

Lord Jesus Christ,
may we sing the song of your praise,
rejoice only in you
live modestly,
abandon our worries
and tell you all our needs,

so that in the refuge of your peace
we can live in the heavenly Jerusalem,
with your help,
who are blessed and glorious
for eternal ages. Amen.

St Anthony, Sermons II/50

You will not be able to carry another's burdens
unless you first lay down your own. Unburden
yourself first to be able to carry another's.

Lord Jesus Christ,
may the shepherds of your Church
watch over the flock of your faithful
   worthily,
so that they may successfully reach you
who are the Easter of all the saints
and blessed through all ages. Amen.

St Anthony, Sermons I/259

Believing, hoping, loving,
with my whole heart,
with my whole mind,
and with my whole strength,
may I be carried to you, beloved Jesus,
as to the goal of all things,
because you alone are sufficient,
you alone are good and pleasing.

Bonaventure, The Tree of Life

Words full of sweetness and forgiveness:
'Father, forgive them!'
Words full of love and grace:
'Today you will be with me in Paradise!'

Say then with much confidence:
'Have pity on me God,
have pity on me
because my soul trusts in you!'

Bonaventure, Tree of Life

If you would be with me, I will be with you.
Our Lord to Elizabeth of Hungary
(A thirteenth-century Franciscan Tertiary)

I'm coming, Lord:
    O wait for me.

All the way to Calvary
    I'm coming, Lord.

However rough the road may be
    to where the seeds of life are stored,
    I'm coming, Lord,
    but wait for me.

Sr Colette, OSC
(A twentieth-century Poor Clare)

MARY, THE MOTHER OF GOD

Francis and Clare were born teachers, teaching us how to love and honour Mary, the Mother of God, to love the glory of God, to reverence creation and, finally, how to die.

Mary, we greet you!
Holy Lady, Queen and Mother of God,
    you are the virgin who has become the
      Church:
    chosen by the most holy Father in
      heaven,
    consecrated by him as a temple
    with his beloved Son and Consoler-Spirit;
    in you was and resides the fullness of
      Grace,
    the One who is all goodness!

Hail, God's Palace!
Hail, God's Tabernacle!
Hail, God's House!
Hail, God's Garment!
Hail, God's Handmaid!

And hail, all you holy virtues
    poured into the hearts of the faithful
    through the grace and light of the Holy
      Spirit,

to turn us from our unbelief
into God's faithful servants!

Francis, Salutation of the Blessed Virgin Mary*

Holy virgin Mary,
among women there is no one like you
born into the world.
You are the daughter and the servant
of the most high and supreme king and
Father of heaven,
you are the mother of our most holy
Lord Jesus Christ,
you are the spouse of the Holy Spirit.
Pray for us
with St Michael the archangel
and all the powers of the heavens
and all the saints,
to your most holy, beloved Son
the Lord and master.

Francis, Antiphon for the Office of the Passion

A Christmas day prayer

We thank you, Holy Father
for in the midst of a frigid winter
you made springtime blossom for us.
During the winter chill
you have given us a breath of spring:
the birth of your Son Jesus.
Today the Virgin has given birth to the Son
of God,

like blessed earth consecrated by the
Father himself,
springing forth with nourishment for
us, repentant sinners.
Today the angels sing: 'Glory to God in the
highest.'
Today silence and peace have returned to
the world.   *St Anthony, Sermons II/122*

We ask you, Our Lady,
who are called the morning star,
dispel with your light
the thick fog which fills my soul.
Like the light of the moon
fill my emptiness, scatter my darkness
so that I may come to the fullness of
eternal life
and the life of never fading glory.
Grant this with the help of him
who was born from you yet who gave
you life.
To him be honour for ever. Amen
    St Anthony, Sermons II/108

Lady and Mother of God,
your name is like a strong tower
in which we find refuge,
a sweet name which comforts us,
a name of blessed hope.

In the recesses of my being
   you are, O Lady.
Your name is like a shining light,
   a sweet taste in the mouth,
      a delightful song in the ears of your
         children.   *St Anthony, Sermons I/162*

A modern prayer to our Lady

Lady, place me with your Son
   dancing or dying.
May his hand be always beneath my head.
A mirror he is to me, the image I would
   become.

Father, place me with your Son,
   dancing or dying.
Spin the great spindle of the dance,
   to twist the thread of the new creation
   as we whirl and twirl
   to the beat of the Spirit's drum . . .

   'til the spindle of the spinning
   and the shuttle of the weaving
   and the drum of the dancing
   fall silent and still
   in the kingdom that is to come.

Place me with your Son,
   dancing and dying. *Sr Frances Teresa, OSC*
      (A twentieth-century Poor Clare)

WONDER AND RESPECT
FOR ALL CREATION

*Over the last century worldwide admiration
for St Francis has grown among Christians
and non-Christians alike. Many have been
captivated by his single-mindedness, joyful-
ness and refusal to be tied down by property
and institutions. His written masterpiece, the*
Canticle of the Sun, *or* Canticle of Brother Sun,
*shows how he identified with the whole of
creation, finding God's presence there as the
inspiration for his life and poverty. Pope John
Paul II proclaimed St Francis the patron saint
of ecologists.*

*This translation of the Canticle of the Sun tries
to catch the poetry and delight rather than to lit-
erally translate the words:*

Praise and glory, honour and blessing
   be yours, O Lord,
   O Most High,
   Most Powerful.

Praise and glory, honour and blessing
   be yours, O Most High.
   O my Lord, be praised.

Let everything you have made
    be a song of praise to you,
    above all, His Excellency the Sun (our
      brother);
    through him you flood our days with light.

He is so beautiful, so radiant, so splendid,
    O Most High, he reminds us of you.

My Lord, be praised
    through our Sister the Moon and through
      each Star.
You made them so clear and precious and
    lovely
    and set them in the heavens for all to
      see.

Through Brother Wind and Sister Water
    be praised, O Lord, be praised.

The Moon and Stars are clear and dear
    and fair,
    through them be praised, and through
      the Clouds and Air
    by which you nourish us each changing
      day;
    through precious Water, pure in every
      way,
    so useful, humble, chaste, receive our
      song.

Through Brother Fire, robust and glad
and strong,
    none shines as he shines in blackest
    night,
    how handsome he, how joyous and how
    bright.
O my Lord, be praised!

Let everything you have made
    be a song of praise to you.
Above all, our Sister, Mother, Lady Earth
    who feeds and rules and guides us.
Through her you give us fruits and flowers
    rich with a million hues.
O my Lord, be praised.

Be praised, my Lord,
    through those who forgive for your
    love,
    through those who are weak,
    in pain, in struggle,
    who endure with peace,
    for you will make them Kings and Queens,
    O Lord Most High.

Through Death, O Lord, be praised,
    through our Sister Death,
    our Sister Death of the body.

No one who lives can escape from Sister
　　Death.
How terrible for those who have already
　　died inside,
　　　happy those whom Sister Death finds
　　　doing Your most holy will,
　　　no further death can harm them.

O praise and bless my Lord,
　　O give thanks to him,
　　and serve him with great humility.

*Recently a son of Francis wrote a similar song
for our own day and called it* The Song of Sister
Energy

Transcendent, limitless, immortal God of
　　the universe,
　　　yours are wisdom, intelligence, order,
　　　　method and logic.
In you alone is their origin
　　and no one is able to know your mind.

Be praised, Lord God, through the brother-
　　hood of creation,
　　and especially Lady Sister Energy,
　　who is throughout the universe and
　　　equivalent to mass
　　by the equation: $E = mc^2$.

She is awe-inspiring and alluring,
of you, the Invisible God, she is the image.

Be praised, Lord God, through Sisters Quasars, Novae and Supernovae,
in distant galaxies you formed them brilliant, majestic and breath-taking.

Be praised, Lord God, through Sister Light,
travelling at a speed of 186,000 miles per second,
by whom the beauty of all creatures is revealed.

Be praised, Lord God, through Brother Quark discovered
among the elementary particles by the light of the electron.

Be praised, Lord God, through Brother DNA, a double helix,
who carries coded genetic information in the cell nucleus.

Be praised, Lord God, through Brother Ocean,
who is wide and deep and teeming with varied fauna and flora.

Be praised, Lord God, through Brothers
    Coal, Oil and Gas,
    and Sisters Nuclear Fusion, Solar and
        Tidal Power,
    by whom you give us light and warmth;
    they are strong and vigorous, depend-
        able and attractive.

Be praised, Lord God, through our Sister
    Mother Earth,
    who had a modest though radiant place
    in the splendour of the expanding
        universe;
    from her evolved the intricate and
        lovely network of matter, life and
        mind.

Be praised, Lord God, through those who
    work for justice and peace.
Blessed are they who serve and support
    the United Nations Organisation,
    for by you, Source of Peace, they shall
        be honoured.

Be praised, Lord God, through our Sister
    Bodily Death,
    who takes us to the next stage of our
        existence.

Woe to those who drive out love and
    destroy the brotherhood of creation.
Blessed are they who love all creatures
    according to your will,
    for they are building the new heaven
        and earth.

Praise and bless the Lord of the universe,
    and give him thanks and serve him with
        great humility.

Eric Doyle, OFM
(A twentieth-century Friar)

God made the atom
    and we have made the atom bomb;
    God made precious stones and metals,
    and we have made weapons of destruction;
    God made fire,
    and we have burned our neighbour;
    God made water,
    and we have produced acid rain;
    God made fresh air,
    and we have invented pollution;
    God made food in abundance,
    and we have created starvation and
        mountains of butter.

God gave us the gift of free will,
   and we have made slaves of ourselves;
God gave us the gift of new, young life,
   and we have produced cosmetics;
God gave us the gift of tears,
   and we have forgotten how to cry;
God gave us the gift of laughter,
   and we laugh together no more;
God gave us the gift of his love,
   before it is too late, please
      let us love.

Sr Leo, OSC
(A twentieth-century Poor Clare)

Praise God for every flowering plant that
   you see.

Clare to her sisters

The person who possesses holy Obedience
   is subject and submissive
   to all persons in the world,
   and not to man only
   but even to all beasts and wild animals,
   so that they may do whatever they want
      with him
   inasmuch as it has been given to them
      from above by the Lord.

Francis, Salutation of the Virtues

Lord, help us to build up a new world
one in which the lion will heal the
wounds of the lamb,
and the serpent dry the tears of the infant.
Help us to build up a world in which
a little girl will caress the lion's mane,
and the leopard and a man will hold
hand and paw,
together proclaiming peace.
Lord, when the serpent injects his poison,
make me honey to counteract it.
When an earthquake opens the ground,
make of me a bamboo ladder stretching
like a bridge
to unite the ledges of the abyss.
When people are invaded by waves of
doubt and anguish,
make of me a safe ship in which to
cross the torrent.

A Christian from Zaïre

Let us be satisfied with humble places.
Grant us to serve without arrogance or
vanity.
Make us at home with the earth, with the
poor and humble.
Teach us how to wait, to listen and to
remain silent.

Make us small and weak, in such a way
that others may even be able to come
to our assistance.

Give us that most beautiful of all privileges:
not to have any privilege.

Send us forth on the highways of the world
to seek your name in all religions,
confessions and creatures.

Hermann Shaluck, OFM
(The previous Minister General of the
Friars Minor)

THE GLORY OF GOD

Francis rejoiced in the wonder and beauty of God, and sang songs and poems which made him one of the first vernacular poets of Italy. In his first Rule for his new brothers, he wrote:

All-powerful, most holy, most high and
supreme God,
holy and just Father,
Lord, King of heaven and earth,
we thank you for yourself,
for through your holy will
and through your only Son
with the Holy Spirit
you have created all things, spiritual
and corporal
and, having made us in your own
image and likeness,
you placed us in paradise.
And through our own fault we have fallen.
And we thank you
for as through your Son you created us,
so also, through your holy love with
which you loved us,
you brought about his birth
as true God and true man

by the glorious, ever-virgin, most blessed
   holy Mary;
and you willed to redeem us captives
through his cross and blood and death.
And we thank you
   for your Son himself who will come again
   in the glory of his majesty . . .

*Francis loved to try and put his perception of
God into words:*

O Lord our God and Son of God
   how holy you are,
      there is no one else who works such
         wonders.
You are strong, mighty,
   above all, and all-powerful.

You are the Father so holy,
   King of heaven and King of earth.
You are three and you are one,
   you are GOD.
You are good: each good and the greatest
   good.
The only God, the true God.

You are love and charity,
   wisdom and humility,
   patience and beauty,
   peace and safety.
You are quietness.

You are joy.
You are our hope and our gladness.
You are justice and judgement,
    strength and discernment.
You are the heart's desire.

You are gentleness and our protector,
    our guardian and our defender,
    our refuge and our strength.

You, you are our faith, our hope and our
    charity,
    our great tenderness.
You are unlimited goodness,
    vast and wonderful.
O Lord, O my God, almighty and merciful,
    O Saviour!   *Francis, The Praises of God,*
                    tr. Sister Frances Teresa, OSC

When you have loved him, you shall be
    chaste,
    when you have touched him, you shall
        become pure,
    when you have accepted him, you shall
        be a virgin,
    whose power is stronger,
    whose generosity more abundant,
    whose appearance more beautiful,
    whose love more tender,
    whose courtesy more gracious.

In whose embrace you are already caught
    up;
  who has adorned your breast with
    precious stones
  and has placed priceless pearls in your
    ears,
  and has surrounded you with sparkling
    gems
  as though with blossoms of springtime,
  and placed on your head a golden
    crown
  as a sign to all of your holiness.
Clare, First letter to Agnes of Prague

Thanks be to God
  through our Lord Jesus Christ
  who has transported us
  out of darkness into his marvellous
    light,
  when through light exteriorly given
  we are disposed to re-enter
  the mirror of our mind, in which divine
    realities shine forth.
Bonaventure, Soul's Journey 2

We can contemplate God not only outside
us and within us, but also above us: outside through traces of him, within through

his image and above through the light which shines upon our minds, which is the light of Eternal Truth, since 'our' mind is formed immediately by Truth itself. Those who have become practised in the first way have already entered the court before the tabernacle; those practised in the second way have entered the sanctuary; those practised in the third way enter with the high priest into the Holy of Holies, where the Cherubim of glory stand over the ark.

Bonaventure, Soul's Journey 5

Lord of my origin,
   draw me closer to you.

Lord of my existence,
   direct all my ways.

Lord of my calling,
   give me strength to go on.

Lord of my faith,
   preserve me from doubt.

Lord of my hope,
   keep me from despair.

Lord of my love,
   let me never grow cold.

Lord of my past,
    may I never forget you.

Lord of my present,
    be near me always.

Lord of my future,
    keep me faithful to the end.

Lord of my life,
    let me live in your presence.

Lord of my death,
    receive me at last.

Lord of my eternity,
    bless me forever. Amen.

Eric Doyle, OFM

'ARROW' PRAYERS

Although the poetic strain in Franciscan prayer sometimes leads to many words, there is also the kind of prayer which sends brief arrows of love and longing to God. Here are some examples of short darts of Franciscan love.

My God and my All.

Who are you, O God, and who am I?

Sing and praise your Creator with a joyful song.

Jesus, Child of Bethlehem.

Our Father who art in heaven.

The Lord is my shepherd, I shall not want.

Let us now begin to serve God,
    for up to now we have done nothing.

Lift up your heart, lift up your heart.

What does my Lord Jesus Christ order me to do?

Place your mind in the mirror of eternity.

Draw me after you!

Kiss me with the happiest kiss of your mouth!

O blessed poverty! O holy poverty! O God-centred
poverty!

CLARE'S ADVICE TO HER SISTERS
Always be lovers of your souls, and those of all
your sisters.
Just have confidence in Christ.
Always remember the blessed water
that came from the right side of our Lord
Jesus Christ
as he hung upon the cross.

LESSONS IN DYING

Francis and Clare teach us how to die

Death is a serious thing. As we get older and inevitably nearer to this event, we realise more strongly than ever, not the terror of death – for we have a merciful God – but the seriousness of this entrance to eternity.

Francis made of his death a carefully prepared liturgy: lying on the bare ground, stripped, the wounds of his stigmata – so long hidden – exposed to all: an icon of the crucified.

Let us each prepare our liturgy for this endless moment, 'sudden and intimate' in Newman's words; for this leap into eternity, made possible for us by Christ's leap into time. 'The hope of eternity crowns our faith in the incarnation' (Cantalamessa).

M. Austin, OSC

Go without anxiety
> for you have a good escort for your
> > journey.
Go, for he who created you has made you
> holy

and has loved you with a tender love,
always protecting you as a mother her
child.
May you be blessed, O Lord,
for having created me.
Clare to herself on her deathbed

Do you see the King of glory whom I see?
Clare to her sisters as she lay dying

Let us now begin to serve God, for up to
now we have done very little.
Francis on his deathbed

THE BLESSING

Finally, they give us their blessing.

May the Lord bless you and keep you.
May he show his face to you and be merciful
    to you.
May he turn his countenance to you and
    give you peace.
May the Lord bless you.

Francis

May the Lord bless you and keep you,
    may he show his face to you and have
        mercy on you.
May he turn his countenance towards you
    and give you peace.

I bless you in my life and after my death,
    as much as I can (and more than I can)
    with every blessing that the Father of
        mercies ever has or ever will have,
    for his blessed sons and daughters,
    in heaven and here on earth,
    every blessing with which a spiritual
        father and mother
    have ever blessed or will bless
    their spiritual sons and daughters.

Always be lovers of your own souls,
 and those of others,
 and always be careful to observe
 what you have promised to the Lord.

May the Lord be with you always and may
 you be with him,
 always and in every place. Amen.

Clare

The Lord bless you.
May he fill your feet with dance
 and your arms with strength.
May he fill your hearts with tenderness
 and your eyes with laughter.
May he fill your ears with music
 and your nose with pleasant scents.
May he fill your mouth with jubilation
 and your heart with joy.
May he give us ever anew the desert graces:
 silence, fresh water and renewed hope.
May he give us all ever anew
 the strength to give hope a new face.
May the Lord bless you. Amen.

Hermann Shaluck, OFM
A blessing for our day

Acknowledgements

All quotations from the writings of Francis are in the translation of Regis Armstrong, OFM Cap, with the exception of those marked with an asterisk which are in the translation of Charles Serignat, OFM Cap.

The publishers wish to express their gratitude to the following for permission to include copyright material in this book:

Paulist Press, 997 Macarthur Blvd., Mahwah, NJ 07430, USA, for the extracts from *Francis and Clare: The Complete Works,* trans. Regis Armstrong, OFM Cap; *Angela of Foligno: Complete Works; Bonaventure: The Soul's Journey into God; The Tree of Life* and *The Life of St Francis* which form part of Paulist Press' series *Classics of Western Spirituality.*

Matthew James Publishing Ltd, 19 Wellington Close, Chelmsford, Essex, CM1 2EE, for the extract from *Praying with Clare and Francis of Assisi,* trans. Charles Serignat, OFM Cap.

Franciscan Press, Quincy University, 1800 College Avenue, Quincy, IL 62301-2699, USA, for the extract from *Omnibus of Sources,* Franciscan Herald Press, Chicago, 1972.